Scrum Essentials

Contents

Your Free Gift

As a thank you for reading *Scrum Essentials*, I would like to give you two free gifts. The first is a copy of *The Scrum Checklist*. In it, you will learn how to get started with Scrum or assess your current implementation of Scrum. It contains a list of guidelines that will help keep you and your team on track.

The second gift is *The Sprint Burndown Template* that allows you to visualize how much work is remaining in a sprint. This burndown chart can be used to communicate the progress of the project to team members, customers, or stakeholders. It's a great way to manage scope and schedules. These gifts are a perfect complement to the book and will help you along your Scrum journey. Visit http://www.linuxtrainingacademy.com/scrum-resources to download your free gifts.

Introduction

Ideas are cheap. A lot of people seem to think that majority of the software development process is just creating a vague concept of an application that people might want. You've probably heard a lot of people say things like, "I have this idea for an app that'll surely reach a million downloads!" only to find their app lost in an ocean of similar apps.

Creating great software and delivering them on time requires a rather systematic but not overly rigid implementation scheme. Quality and time must go together. If you deliver software that's full of bugs or poor in user experience, you really can't expect another transaction with your client. A lot of programmers fear this outcome and instead take too long to create programs.

You have a limited amount of time to create software,

especially when you're given a deadline, self-imposed or not. You'll want to make sure that the software you build is at least decent but more importantly, on time. How do you balance quality with time?

The Fall of the Waterfall Methodology

One of the oldest ways to create software is called "The Waterfall". This method forces the programmers to concretize the software ideas. It starts off with a planning phase wherein the people intricately write down everything about the software about to be built. All the necessary steps to be taken are documented and the team creates an estimate as to how long it would take for the software to be ready. The stakeholders then check the plan. Once their approval is met, the programmers begin their work. This methodology is called "The Waterfall" because when teams complete their assigned work, they pass it on to the next team. When everything is done, the software is thoroughly tested and then handed off to the client or customer.

The problem with this method is its rigidity and tediousness. Everything has to be written down, with assumptions pretty much set in stone and plans that have to be followed exactly. Have you ever noticed that when you try to estimate how long something would take, sometimes the result would actually be twice, trice, or even quadruple your assumption? Take this phenomenon and apply it to a huge project and you've got a very expensive disaster waiting to happen.

Another problem is that this method assumes that all the necessary features of the software are already thought of at the beginning of the development cycle. When you write a letter to someone, do you write exactly the things you initially thought of before writing the letter, or do you incorporate a lot of new thoughts as you write? Which one would've turned out better? Imagine not being able to change whatever you plan on writing. That'd be disastrous! The same is true with the Waterfall methodology, which is why a lot of companies have been trying to find different methodologies in creating software.

What is Scrum?

Scrum is a boon to companies that are struggling to follow the Waterfall methodology or aren't even following a software development methodology at all. It's a framework that makes creating complex software and delivering it on time a lot easier.

Scrum is easy to understand, but it can take a few years to actually master. This shouldn't discourage you though; the benefits far outweigh the learning curve.

Scrum has been in use since the early 1990s and is now gaining even more popularity. As I've mentioned before, Scrum isn't a methodology; it's a framework within the Agile Software Development methodology that helps you create great software with a set of guidelines and roles for people to follow.

The Scrum framework makes use of Scrum Teams, which are groups of people with specified roles. Scrum takes into account the fact that the people creating the software are human – they make mistakes, think of new ideas along the way, and more. While one might think that this would lead to missing product deadlines and more bugs, it actually helps avoid these problems.

Since the Scrum framework is a subset of the Agile Software Development methodology, the principles of the agile approach also apply. First you create a product backlog, which is a set of features obtained from potential users, officemates, and other people relevant to the product. Think of it somewhat like an app request list; it contains features that may make the product more profitable. The product backlog is a prioritized list, which means that you have to work on either the most important or the most urgent items first. This makes sure that you don't spend countless hours or days on expendable features while skimping on the important ones.

While the human mind in itself is very powerful, it can't handle huge and complex tasks; it prefers short bursts of simple tasks. This is why the work is performed in short iterations that can be as short as a week to a month. This is often called a sprint.

At the end of the sprint, there should be a ready-to-ship product. Features in the sprint that come out late are early markers that there is a bottleneck in operations and have to be remedied quickly. You can think of sprints as mini milestones. The team reviews the end product and shown to the stakeholders to get their feedback. Based on that feedback they can make the necessary changes to the whole product backlog or to the next sprints. For example, if it turns out that a certain feature was causing more trouble than it's worth, the team could decide to trash that feature and make the necessary changes. Should they think of new features to add, they could easily add those to the backlog and create a rough estimate of how long it'd take and adjust the product timeline accordingly.

The good thing about having sprints is that every sprint has a ready-to-ship product, so if the next sprint results in a very buggy and unstable software, the team could just revert to the last milestone and not have to start from scratch.

While Scrum is usually used in software development, a lot of the concepts in it could be used for other types of products or even work. Scrum takes the human tendency into account and creates very sustainable workflows.

What is Agile Software Development?

As I've mentioned before, Scrum is a subset of the Agile software development methodology. It takes a more human approach to solving problems. Instead of wasting time creating long, intricate documentations that nobody really takes time to read properly anyway, Agile helps people get right into writing code. It also considers customer input even in the middle of the development cycle, as opposed to one-sided inputs from the team at the beginning of the development cycle.

What is the Difference between Scrum and Agile Software Development?

Since Scrum is a subset of the Agile software development methodology, the two really shouldn't be compared.

In Scrum, teams deal with sprints. Short meetings are held wherein the team decides which features in the product backlog make it into the sprints. They also decide who works on the sprint and how long each task would take. Members usually talk about tasks they're planning on doing for that day, tasks they're currently working on, and problems they're having with certain tasks. When the sprint ends, there is a review or retrospective meeting wherein the team talks about the progress of the software being developed. They make necessary changes to the succeeding sprints depending on the features that need to be added or removed and the time constraint.

In the Agile software development methodology, iterations include planning, design, coding, testing, etc. This means that in each iteration, a fully working product should be ready and can be presented to the stakeholders.

Scrum sprints should roughly correspond to iterations in agile because sprints also require having working, ready-to-ship prototypes. In a nutshell, Agile is a set of guidelines to help with software development, whereas Scrum is an implementation of those guidelines specifically to help with project management.

Why Use Scrum?

Oftentimes, a lot of startup software companies struggle to deliver working prototypes on time. Products often come out unsatisfactorily. If they even come out on time, they often lack a lot of important features. Chaos ensues, as programmers do not have specific deadlines on small tasks such that they become complacent. They underestimate huge tasks and only focus on them as the deadline approaches. They then discover a lot of overwhelming problems that make them miss the deadline or deliver spaghetti code.

The nightmare does not have to go on forever. Companies that have started using Scrum have noticed significant changes in product quality and timeliness. The programmers are more productive as tasks are split into small manageable pieces. The software could easily be changed to suit the ever-changing needs of the client or the user. Instead of just creating features that companies imagine users will want, they actually get to have input from them and actually incorporate them into the software. More frequent releases also mean improved return on investment and stability.

Consider the Truth

Scrum is a great framework, but it isn't a magic spell that automatically fixes everything. It can, however, help you handle complex software development.

The Scrum framework is easy to learn, but it can be quite difficult to apply. It doesn't exactly offer a rigid set of instructions for you to follow, so a lot of estimations and predictions will still come from you. It doesn't tell you exactly what you should do to make great software, but it lets you see possible kinks in your plans so you don't end up wasting valuable company time and money.

In the succeeding chapters, you'll learn more about how Scrum works. You'll be equipped with the essential tools so you can learn to use Scrum in the right context.

Scrum Roles

In the Scrum framework, there are three major roles: the product owner, the Scrum master, and the team members. Let's go through each one:

The product owner acts somewhat like a middleman, taking all the necessary steps to ensure that the customer or client gets what they want while also making sure that the team members and stake holders know what to do. The product owner gets inputs from both sides and chooses carefully what gets added to the prioritized list for product development.

The Scrum Master's role is probably the most important in the software development process. The Scrum master makes sure that everyone is doing his job properly and nobody's falling behind. The job of the Scrum master is not to boss people around, but to actually guide the team in applying the concepts of Scrum. This is important, especially for companies that are still adjusting to the concept of Agile. Scrum masters have to be vigilant in searching for possible impediments that arise.

Scrum makes a lot of potential problems easily visible and it's the job of the Scrum master to make sure that the team takes the appropriate steps to solve the problems before they go out of hand. While one might think that Scrum masters and product owners should be the same thing, it really shouldn't; a lot of times product owners may push too many tasks onto the team that could cause a product to be delivered late and it's the job of the Scrum master to negotiate and push back some changes that may lead to the project's demise. This can't be done if the product owner and the Scrum master is one person.

While Scrum masters seem like project managers at times, Scrum masters don't exactly tell people what to do. They're not allowed to micromanage team members.

The team members are the developers in the software development process. They take responsibility in choosing tasks they can handle and do them in the most efficient way possible. The number of team members could be as small as three to as large as even twenty (though one would question the efficiency of having too much people in a group). These team members are typically comprised of software developers, user interface designers, testers and debuggers, etc. The team members communicate with the product owner and scrum master so that they can get as much valuable input as they can.

To maximize the efficiency of the team, team members are typically assigned one task at a time. Multitasking reduces the efficiency of the team as a whole and would often lead to lower-quality deliverables.

Getting Started in Scrum

The first step taken in Scrum is to make clear what the end product is supposed to be like. That's the job of the product owner. However, instead of a long, boring documentation with a rigid set of specifications, a prioritized list is created with the most important features (as determined by customers, clients, team members, Scrum master, and the product owner) at the top of the list. As I've mentioned before, this is what's called a product backlog. Unlike documentations, product backlogs are clear and concise, but give more freedom to the developers and won't cause as much delay as the Waterfall methodology should a team member fail to deliver.

The product backlog acts like a product blueprint, filled with features that would theoretically make the product great. This blueprint is not set in stone, so any new features that the Scrum master, team members, and product owner agree on can be added to it.

The product backlog not only includes the features of the software being developed, but it also could contain research and debugging tasks related to making the product ready-to-ship and profitable.

If you're a bit familiar with the concept of product backlogs, you may have heard of the term "user stories". This is the most common way of writing features into the product backlog. Instead of just creating tasks, it becomes like a mini-essay as to why a certain feature should be added, fixed, or removed and what the end user would get in return.

When tasks are created in the product backlog, the team creates estimates on how long each task would take and how hard they'd be. This'll make prioritization of tasks a lot easier for the product owner. Unit-less points are used to rate the difficulty of tasks because it's difficult to predict how long something would take if you haven't even started doing it. Over the course of the project, however, when the team starts to get insights on some of the tasks, they could create estimates as to how long each point corresponds to and therefore create a good estimation as to when the product creation would finish. This'll allow the product owner to make necessary changes, like removing certain features, so that they can make sure that the product is delivered on time with the necessary features.

Since one of the main concepts of Scrum is to split complex tasks into manageable and smaller tasks, larger tasks in the product backlog will be split into smaller tasks. Small tasks that may be too simple on their own may be consolidated into other tasks as well. This is done during the Sprint planning meeting.

Tasks in the product backlog should not be too detailed, but they shouldn't be too general as well. Tasks written should contain important bits of information while allowing the developer a certain degree of freedom. The task simply needs to be described well enough to be able to tell if it is completed or not. In short, keep it as short as possible while retaining the important details.

The product owner's task is to check the product backlog regularly and update it should there be necessary changes to be done to the end product. This is often caused by new requests from the client, new discoveries along the development, new competitors that would render the current product obsolete, potential problems, etc.

Chapter Summary

The roles implemented in scrum make it possible for every person to be more responsible in making decisions. Certain restrictions are set even for product owners to avoid unhealthy biases, work overload, and unrealistic goals. In the next chapter we'll talk more about what happens inside sprints, which are one of the main highlights of the Scrum framework.

All About Sprints

Before we get further into Scrum, let's dig a little deeper into what a sprint really is.

What is a Sprint?

Sprints work like mini-milestones, hence they would not typically take longer than a month. At the end of the sprint, the Scrum team should already have a minimum viable product to show to the client or customer.

While Scrum is one of the most flexible frameworks available, there still has to be a certain amount of rigidity to maintain order in the development process. This is the reason why sprints have fixed beginning and end dates, having more or less the same duration. Changes that need to be performed will be done in the next sprint if another sprint is already running. This, of course, assumes that work is done in ideal conditions wherein changes that pop-up over the course of the software development wouldn't significantly affect the work already being done. Unfortunately, a there's a lot of non-idealities in the business setting. Should there be huge changes that would render the current tasks in the sprint useless, the current sprint is stopped.

Sprint Planning

A Sprint planning meeting is held before each sprint begins. The product owner and the Scrum team take a look at what's in the product backlog. They look at the tasks in the product backlog and discuss the goals regarding the software they're developing. This helps the Scrum team build software closer to what the client or customer wants.

After getting an overview of the software in development, the Scrum team chooses tasks from the product backlog that will make it into the sprint. The tasks with the highest priority will make it first into the sprint. The team members are the ones who decide how much work they're planning to do; therefore, the team will have full accountability. The product owner has no control over how much the team puts into one sprint, but since he gets to dictate the order of the tasks in the product backlog, he can be assured that the most important items on the list are done first. The team can put lower priority items on a sprint as well, but this is usually due to the feature being a prerequisite for another higher priority feature.

Sprint-planning meetings can last for a few hours because this is the phase wherein the team members are deciding how their next couple of days would go. They'll compute how much work they can do in a day and therefore, choose tasks that would fit into their work schedule. This has to be carefully done to avoid burnouts and late delivery of code.

Before the team members can choose the tasks, the amount of available time still has to be determined. Team members work together to find out how much accumulated time they have to work on the sprint. The team then gets the most important tasks on the product backlog, splits them into tasks, and puts them into a sprint backlog. The team members could then choose the tasks they'll do. Should there be tasks dependent on the accomplishment of another task, the team will work together to make sure that they won't run into a problem of spending hours just waiting for another member to finish his code. They'll also make sure that each team member doesn't get too much or too little work to do.

The process of breaking down tasks into smaller tasks and putting them on a sprint backlog still involves the need to communicate with the product owner. The team verifies certain tasks to make sure that they're on the right track. They repeat this process of breaking down tasks and then verifying them with the product owner until they use up all of their estimated available hours.

The end result of this meeting is a concrete list of things to do, with people assigned to do specific tasks. Each task will have an estimated time of completion, which is typically in hours since tasks that take more than a day to do are split into smaller tasks.

The team can use a huge whiteboard filled with Post-It notes in different colors to indicate whether the tasks have been started, are already being done, are currently being verified, and are completed. This method is often seen as obsolete though. A lot of companies are now investing in tools that help Scrum teams visualize their tasks.

While Agile is a lot more flexible than Waterfall, sprints typically don't allow changes to be made. Should the product owner want to add a new feature or task in the middle of the sprint, the team would put it in the product backlog and perhaps implement it in the next sprint. Should there be any major changes that change the tasks' order of importance, the product owner can stop the sprint. When the sprint is stopped, the team stops whatever tasks they're working on, go back to the product backlog, and start another sprint planning meeting. Stopping sprints should be a rare circumstance. If the product owner keeps on stopping sprints, the development process becomes very counterproductive and will inevitably lead to incomplete or rushed products.

The good thing about the sprints not being changeable, only stoppable, is that the product owner and the team are forced to think thoroughly about the tasks they put in each sprint. Since during each sprint, no changes are allowed, the team could focus on their assigned tasks without fear that their tasks would change.

While one might think that the product owner is at a disadvantageous position due to not being able to make as much decisions as usual product managers, product owners are actually benefitting from this. First off, since the team decides on how long tasks would take and which one they're planning to work on, they get accountability for their work and the headache of assigning tasks and micromanagement is no longer present. Also, people tend to work better if they get to choose the tasks themselves.

Another benefit that product owners get is that they could implement changes they want and put them in the product backlog. Since the product backlog is a prioritized list, the product owner can be sure that the tasks he wants done first will most likely be done first. Unlike a lot of rigid methodologies that don't allow changes in specs and features in the middle of the development, Scrum allows product owners to make changes in-between sprint cycles.

Sprint Execution

After planning what tasks go into the next sprint, the Scrum team starts doing their designated work to finish the features indicated in the current sprint. Whether a certain feature is finished or not will depend on whether the team is confident that the feature is ready to be integrated into the product to be released at the end of the sprint.

Since the team members get a high degree of freedom in estimating the amount of time it takes for tasks to finish and even in choosing the tasks they're going to do based on their free work hours, they're also free to choose which tasks they're going to do first from the sprint backlog provided that there are no dependencies that force them to work sequentially.

The Daily Scrum

When the sprint starts, the Team holds another meeting that's one of the key concepts of Scrum. This meeting isn't as long as the Sprint planning meeting – it only takes about 15 minutes or less to complete. This meeting is called the Daily Scrum. Every workday at a specific time, everyone on the scrum team is required to attend this short meeting. Since this meeting is meant to be brief, the team members hold the meeting standing up. Every team member gets to talk about what they've already accomplished, what they're planning to accomplish for the day, and what their impediments are.

The Scrum master takes note of what the team members say and helps them resolve any issue that's preventing them from doing their tasks at hand after the meeting. The Daily Scrum does not allow discussions to happen, as that would make the meeting a lot longer than it needs to be. Any discussions that need to take place will happen after the meeting so that other team members not concerned can get to work immediately. Other people, like the product owner and stakeholders, could attend the Daily Scrum, but they're discouraged from interrupting team members to ask questions or start a discussion during the meeting.

In the Daily Scrum, the team members aren't really reporting to the Scrum master, but to each other. While they can let the product owners join their meeting to give them an overview on what's already happened and what's about to happen, this isn't a requirement.

After the Daily Scrum, team members change the amount of time they have in the tasks they're currently doing on the sprint backlog. After each team member has updated their tasks, the Scrum master combines the number of hours left for the whole sprint and plots it on the Sprint Burndown Chart. This is perhaps one of the biggest highlights of the Scrum framework because it allows the team to see whether they're about to be late or not in delivering the product.

The Sprint Burndown Chart shows how much work is left each day until the sprint ends. As the days pass, there'll be a downward slope that can be seen on the chart that'll eventually hit zero, indicating that the sprint has ended. The chart shows how much progress the team is making by showing how much hours of work they have left. Should the team notice that the slope of the graph is not approaching zero on their projected deadline, they can speed up their work or make necessary changes to accomplish their tasks. This is an important feature of the Scrum framework because it allows teams to visualize the amount of time it takes to finish the product and take necessary steps to make sure that it gets delivered on time.

Potentially Shippable Product Increment

As I've mentioned before, at the end of the sprint, the team is supposed to have a minimum viable product that they can present to the client or the customer. This minimum viable product is considered a potentially shippable product increment. This means that the product, based on the specifications agreed upon by the Scrum team members, is ready to be presented to the client or customer.

What would it take for a product to be potentially shippable though? In most cases, the product has to be well tested, well documented, and can actually be a standalone, albeit bare-minimum product.

Even if the product finished in sprints are "potentially shippable", it doesn't mean that it actually should be shipped. A program could be bug free, well documented, and have basic functionality that allows it to stand on its own, but it doesn't mean that it people would actually buy it. Furthermore, clients that have requested complex software would most likely not accept a program with minimal features. The term "potentially shippable" just means that you already have a concrete proof of your progress that you can show to a customer or client. These sprint products also act as "save points" that allow you to revert to the last stable build of your software should there be unforeseen bugs that surface in the last sprint.

To make it simple, imagine having a very complex game that you have to create. In the first sprint, the team works on collision detection, save functionality, and other basic functions that would allow the client or customer to get a glimpse on what the game is about. In this sprint, however, the game sprites (in this context, sprites are graphic elements like the character avatar, environment, etc.) have not been included yet and the game just has a couple of vague shapes to represent the characters and some important artifacts. At the end of the sprint, your team would have come up with a potentially shippable product, but it's definitely something you're not going to want to release to gamers. In this case, potentially shippable products mean products that have completely working specific functionality.

Sprint Review

When the sprint ends, there'll be two more activities that need to be done to check the overall state of the product and make necessary changes. First, we'll talk about the sprint review.

In the sprint review, other people outside the Scrum team are invited. Customers, clients, stakeholders, and other people relevant to the software development process will communicate with each other to review the features completed in the sprint that has just finished. Rather than view the sprint independently, people in the sprint review view the finished sprint in the context of the whole development process. Compared to daily Scrum meetings that don't allow collaboration and brainstorming to happen, sprint reviews allow everyone to see what's really happening with the current product. They could give suggestions for the next phases of software development to make sure that the best possible steps are taken.

Sprint reviews allow people outside the team to get a better understanding of what's going on in the development process. This allows them to help guide the Scrum team in the right direction should there be oversights. The Scrum team also gets a better understanding on how the business side of the development process works. This will help Scrum team members make more economically viable decisions.

The main point of sprint reviews is to be able to look at the product and the features it now has. People with different roles get to offer different insights in order to achieve a centralized goal.

Sprint Retrospective

The second activity done when a sprint finishes is called the sprint retrospective.

While the sprint review focuses on the product, the sprint retrospective focuses on the procedures and tasks done. Since the sprint retrospective is focused on the processes involved in creating the product, people who aren't involved in the technical side of the development process won't be needed in the meeting.

In the sprint retrospective, the Scrum master, product owner, and the scrum team talk about tasks that are a bit problematic and needs changes. If you recall, in the daily scrum team members also talk about what their impediments were in achieving a task. In the sprint retrospective, the team talks about impediments that cause continuous problems in the software development process and what improvements can be implemented.

Starting the Next Sprint

Before starting the next sprint, the product owner takes all the changes that were made during the sprint review meeting and the sprint retrospective meeting, as well as the necessary changes that could have appeared in the middle of the sprint cycle, into the product backlog. The product owner basically updates the product backlog, deleting tasks that are no longer relevant, adding tasks that were suggested by the Scrum team, reordering tasks should there be a change in priority, etc. After that, a new sprint cycle is ready to start, with the sprint-planning meeting.

Sprint cycles don't have long downtimes. In most cases, sprint cycles will only have a few hours in between them. Sprints are appropriately named because they are paced fast enough for the development team to be able to work with intense focus. The breaks in-between are long enough for the team members to catch their breath, but not long enough for them to fall behind.

Release Planning

As I've mentioned before, products at the end of the sprint are should not necessarily be already shipped to the client or customer. The product owner decides when the product is going to be ready to be shipped. Should the product owner decide that the features are in the software being built are good enough for delivery, another sprint is done for refactoring, revamps, integration, and testing in order to fully prepare the software for shipment. An analogy could be made to creating a complex essay. You'll have plenty of points to cover and you may decide to split them into smaller bits so that it doesn't overwhelm you, but when you finally finish all the subtopics you'll run through the whole essay to make sure that the thought is coherent and that there's an appropriate structure followed.

The reason why something so adaptive can still be on time in delivering products is that instead of the team and the product owner picking their brains out trying to come up with specifics regarding software development, they come up with more generalized models that they update along the way.

If the product has a fixed release date, the team will try to squeeze in as much sprints as they can while including as much of the necessary features as possible. In other cases, sprints take a bit more relaxed position as the product is only released when the necessary features have been implemented. In both cases, however, the customer or client already has a working product at the end of each sprint.

Common Challenges

Scrum allows the team to find kinks in the development process that may be hampering with the team's progress. For example, in a given sprint, if a team member consistently fails to do his task on time, it'll reflect on the backlogs. Whether it's due to poor time estimation or even lack of skill, Scrum will eventually bring that into surface, allowing the team to take the necessary steps to ensure that the next sprint happens more smoothly than the last.

Scrum makes every team member more responsible since a lot of problems they have would most likely be reflected visually in charts and backlogs. While this may discourage some team members at first, in the long run it helps the team improve as a whole and make the members more accountable to their own decisions. It teaches team members to be relatively independent.

The problem with the flexibility of Scrum is that team

members may unconsciously manipulate the framework instead of striving to improve and find real solutions to the problems at hand. For example, if team members fail to make realistic estimates to the task at hand, instead of striving to make more accurate predictions through experimentation, they may just change the next sprint durations to allow more room for mistakes. This is why highly trained Scrum masters are needed – Scrum in itself is a great tool in delivering robust products on time, but if an inefficient team decides to use it without guidance, they may end up twisting the principles to suit their weaknesses.

A lot of teams struggle with Scrum on the fist try, but eventually they learn to love it. Scrum may be difficult to master, but what it does to the product development process definitely outweighs the effort needed to learn and implement it.

Chapter Summary

Sprints allow a relatively higher degree of freedom than most software development methodologies do. The cost of this freedom is larger room for human error. The concept of Sprint is pretty simple when you think about it – grab the most important tasks in the product backlog that will combine to create a potentially shippable product by the end of the sprint, meet every day and talk about the individual progress of each member, work, update the sprint backlogs, and monitor progress until the sprint cycle is over. What makes it hard is the fact that every person will have different perspectives and way on doing things. This is why Scrum is hard to master and why it's important for teams to stick together. In the next chapter we'll talk about the tools used in Scrum.

Scrum Artifacts

The artifacts of Scrum make a lot of technical procedures in product development more transparent, henceforth allowing a lot of positive changes to happen. By making it clear to everyone what is happening to the product being developed, people from different fields get to contribute better. Here are some of the Scrum artifacts:

Product Backlog

The product backlog has been mentioned a couple of times before, but to make the concept easier to understand it's crucial to emphasize this point – product backlogs are ordered lists of things that a product might need to make it "sellable". The product owner is in charge of creating and modifying this to make sure that the product is created with the most important features put in first.

The product backlog is very dynamic in the sense that it continuously changes throughout the software development process. Since most programs get updated frequently, the product backlog always has something new implemented every now and then. The first product backlog would have relatively crude items, especially if not a lot is known about the specifics in creating the product itself. For example, if a startup company decides on making a game without knowledge on game engines, they might put general tasks like "create something that detects when two items bump into each other". These tasks may be updated throughout the software development when the team has gathered more knowledge about the specifics of game development. While the product is still being used and updated, the product backlog will remain active and will have ever-changing tasks.

Since a potentially shippable product is available after every sprint, should the product owner decide to release the product, the team gets to have feedback from the client or customers, therefore leading to more things being added to the product backlog. Also, the Scrum team or the product owner could find new competitors that would force them to add new features or modify existing ones to keep themselves ahead of the game. Whatever the case, the product backlog always changes.

Since a lot of product backlogs start off with relatively crude and general information, it'll be continuously updated to become more specific. This is done by adding more specific information to certain tasks and more accurate estimates as to how long the tasks would take. Since the product backlog is an ordered list, priority of tasks may also change as needed.

A common pitfall is that teams would take unusually long in refining the product backlog because they were adding unnecessary details to the tasks. One must remember that one of the key aspects of Scrum is task description brevity. The art of putting all the necessary details without going off in tangents and falling into rabbit holes takes time to master. People who use Scrum for a long time eventually make better descriptions of tasks while creating more accurate estimates.

In most cases, the more important items in the product backlog should have more details because they're the ones closest to the next sprint. The items with lower priority will have fewer details, but not necessarily be very vague points. High priority items have to be refined first so that the team can more easily project more accurate timeliness. Refining tasks in the product backlog arbitrarily is discouraged unless you're planning to finish refining them all in one session.

While the Scrum team is responsible for making the estimates regarding task difficulty in terms of time or points, the product owner may help them make more accurate predictions by giving helping them understand opportunity costs and other necessary terms to make good predictions.

Progress Tracking

Even in the middle of a sprint, the total amount of time remaining to finish the product can be seen visually. The product owner takes note of this, usually every sprint review. This data is made available to all stakeholders because of the transparency being a key concept in Scrum.

One of the main reasons why Scrum helps teams deliver great software on time is the way product release dates are forecasted. We'll talk more about the tools used to analyze and predict product release dates and overall progress.

Sprint Backlog

I've mentioned sprint backlogs before as subsets of the product backlog. Another way to think about sprint backlogs is to consider them a prediction on what the next product milestone should be and the necessary steps to take in order to reach that milestone.

While the product owner and other people outside the development team cannot make changes to sprint backlogs (except full termination), the development team can make changes they deem necessary. Should they discover the need to add new tasks to accomplish existing tasks on the sprint backlog, they'll do so. They could also remove tasks that could have become redundant during the sprint cycle.

When the team accomplishes tasks in the sprint backlog, the number of hours remaining for the sprint is updated. The sprint backlog is a great tool for development teams to visualize their progress. Potential delays could more easily be remedied and Scrum teams could gauge how much work they'll have to squeeze in to finish certain tasks.

The great thing about sprints is that even while they're happening, you can see the total amount of work that still needs to be done. Even if some tasks are not yet finished, team members could just update the number of hours remaining to reflect their progress. This is an important aspect of sprints because daily Scrum meetings often require estimates as to how much work is already done and how much work still needs to be done. When enough data is gathered, the team could make accurate predictions as to when the sprint will finish and make adjustments they deem necessary, like speeding up or removing tasks in case the team is falling behind. This makes progress tracking more manageable and more efficient.

Importance of Transparency in Scrum

Transparency is one of the key aspects of Scrum. The development process is made as clear as possible to people involved so that the best possible decisions can be made. A lot of problems in product development come from inaccurate projections and estimations brought about by poor knowledge of the artifacts.

Should full transparency be impossible to attain, the Scrum master has to exert more effort into making sure that people involved in the software development process makes the right decisions. In most cases, however, the Scrum master should inspect the artifacts and be vigilant in detecting discrepancies with what was promised and what was actually done. To make sure that the artifacts are indeed transparent, the Scrum master, product owner, Scrum team, and other relevant people have to work together in understanding the artifacts. Should insufficient transparency be detected, the Scrum master and the team have to work together to increase the transparency of the artifacts.

Completed – What Does it Really Mean?

I've talked about potentially shippable product increments

before, now let's have a more rigorous discussion regarding the perception of completed work.

As a recap, potentially shippable products are products that are completed from sprint cycles. In order to be truly completed though, everyone must agree on standard conditions on what completed work really means. One member may view completed work as something that just works whereas another member may view completed work as something that works, has proper documentation, and thorough testing. If team members don't have a unified idea on what completed tasks should be, the performance of the whole team will inevitably decline.

Remember that potentially shippable products should have the features promised at the start of the sprint such that the product owner could release it. Having a unified concept on what completed tasks are will help teams speed up their work should there be a need to rush a sprint cycle. By standardizing the concept of completed work, teams could aim for a standard minimum to achieve so that at the end of the sprint, all the features needed are present in the product. Having a unified definition of completed work is especially important if multiple Scrum teams are working on one project.

While there's always a potentially shippable product ready at the end of the sprint cycle, it doesn't mean that the features of one sprint are being developed independently from the features of another sprint. It's appropriately called "potentially shippable product increment" because the product grows after each sprint cycle, and every feature added must work well together. Thorough testing is recommended to ensure that new features don't break existing ones.

The idea on what's completed and what isn't is a hard one to standardize. People in the mediocre side tend to be more complacent, whereas people in the perfectionist side tend to be more strict and rigid. Their ideas on what "completed" means will not always coincide, which is why the team needs to work together to have a unified definition of the concept.

A unified idea of completion is not something that's achieved overnight, but as teams work on more projects together, soon enough they'll have a better grasp on what completed tasks should really look like.

Scrum Tools of Communication

1. Burn down chart

We've glanced upon the concept of burn down charts before, but now that we have a deeper understanding on the important concepts of Scrum. So, let's have a more rigorous discussion on this vital tool of communication.

Sprint backlogs get updated everyday to reflect the amount of work remaining in designated tasks. By adding the remaining amount of work from each task, we get the total amount of work remaining for the whole sprint. The total amount of work remaining for the whole sprint is then shown visually using the burn down chart.

Burn down charts typically trend towards zero, as each task gets tackled even just a little bit everyday. Sometimes, however, the amount of work remaining on the previous day may actually be less than that of the work remaining for the next day. This usually happens when there is an error in estimating the amount of work that needs to be done to complete a feature. Some people may get a bit confused because the team worked on a lot of features on the previous day, only to find out that the amount of work remaining on the next day is still the same. This is still a result in underestimating the time it takes to finish certain features. This error may not always be avoidable, especially if the team is not all that familiar with some of the product features to be created.

While the product owner typically cannot just add new tasks to the sprint backlog in the middle of the sprint cycle, team members may choose to add tasks that they find are actually connected to the features they're working on in the current sprint. While typically changes in the sprint cycle is discouraged, if it turns out that the team accidentally left out a feature in the product backlog that's actually needed for a certain feature to work in the current sprint cycle, then by all means the team should add that task and adjust the remaining amount of work remaining for the whole sprint.

A potential problem that arises is when teams fall into the pitfall of grabbing too many tasks from the product backlog that may not actually be necessary, therefore increasing the chances of releasing a potentially shippable product late. Like having a unified idea of completeness, the team should also have a unified idea on what's necessary. What's great about being able to add tasks to the sprint backlog as necessary is that work becomes much more realistic than other methodologies that only allow changes to happen in before product development starts. Allowing necessary changes to happen even in the middle of a product cycle will result in better-built programs.

There are actually two types of burn down charts: release burn down charts and sprint burn down charts. As you might have guessed, release burn down charts show the amount of work remaining for the whole project whereas sprint burn down charts show the amount of work remaining for the current sprint cycle. One can think of release burn down charts as "zoomed-out" versions of sprint burn down charts. Sprint burn down charts are the ones updated daily whereas release burn down charts are usually updated only when sprints are completed.

Release burn down charts allow the team to see whether the product being developed will be released on time or not. If the product is in danger of being released late, the team will have to make necessary adjustments, whether it means working faster or removing certain tasks from the sprint backlog. Sprint burn down charts allow the team to see whether a potentially shippable product is ready at the end of the sprint cycle or not. Like release burn down charts, should they notice a potential delay in release, they'll have to either work faster; but unlike release burn down charts, they most likely cannot just remove tasks from the sprint backlog.

In either case, burn down charts are very useful in predicting the possible release of the product being developed. The more work days that have elapsed, the more accurate predictions can be made. Using the same charts, the team could also create target number of hours in each day to make sure the product is released on time. Saying "we'll need to finish x amount of work in the next sprints to release the product on time" is a lot better than saying the non-constructive "we're going to be late!" statement.

If you've noticed, the charts and logs used always show the time remaining rather than just time elapsed working on the product. In most cases, time elapsed is useless data because time spent working on something does not exactly reflect the amount of concentrated work done. It could also lead to a false sense of accomplishment (teams could mistakenly correlate elapsed work hours with completed work). By instead showing the amount of work that's still unfinished, the team can have a more accurate gauge on the remaining work they still have to do and spread them out evenly.

2. Burn Up Chart

The problem with burn down charts is that they don't show scope changes very clearly. Scope change is when tasks are either added or removed in the product backlog or sprint backlog. This usually happens when the team discovers tasks that actually need to be done prior to other already planned task. Clients, customers, and product owners may also think of additional features along the way. Burn down charts may oversimplify data and lead to estimation and prediction problems in the future.

A burn up chart shows the work that is already completed and the total work with separate data points, as compared to the burn down chart, which combines the two. The total work data will show the amount of work available, which may change as tasks are added or removed. The work that's already completed will show the amount of work that's been done. As I've mentioned before, in burn down charts you may see past days that contain less work to be done than succeeding days, and that's often because of added tasks. Burn up charts show these added tasks clearly, as well as any removed tasks. They also make it easier to see why products take too long to finish or if too much tasks are added.

Just as burn down charts could be represented in hours spent or in story points, burn up charts could also be represented in these two modes. You can use either, depending on whether you're particular about the hours spent in tasks or not.

Burn up charts and burn down charts both have their pros and cons – burn down charts are much simpler to create but won't really tell you as much things as burn up charts will. Burn up charts will, for example, show you that the team had to remove tasks in order to finish a sprint, while burn down charts will only show a sudden downward fall in work remaining.

3. Task board

The task board is a visual representation of the progress of the sprint backlog. In a glance, you'd be able to tell the progress of the tasks quite easily. Team members will update the task board all throughout the sprint. This is where tasks are either added or removed as necessary. The amount of work remaining is then updated in the daily scrum and will be reflected in the burn up or burn down charts.

In task boards, product backlog features to be tackled in the sprint is updated to have more details, with mini-tasks necessary to accomplish the tasks. The columns usually used in the task board are:

- **To Do:** All uncompleted work generally starts here. Team members choose tasks to work on in this column and move them to the "Work in progress" column.
- **Work In Process:** All uncompleted work that people are already working on generally goes here.
- **To Verify:** If there are no separate tasks in testing the completed work, the theoretically-completed work is generally placed here to be verified usually by the Scrum Master or other team members.
- **Completed:** Tasks that have been verified are moved to this column.

Chapter Summary

We've talked about the artifacts of Scrum and the tools of communication used. Remember that Scrum is known for taking into account possible changes in product development, requests of clients or even the product owner, mistakes of the team, and more. The artifacts and tools given here are presented in such a way that a few changes in product features won't completely change the direction of the product or cause significant delay. Sprints should take into account the skills of the team and inputs from various meetings held, instead of sticking to a rigid, specific set of rules. Scrum teams will have different sets of abilities and skills, so feel free to modify the artifacts and tools presented if doing so leads to better results.

Conclusion

Scrum can help teams deliver great products on time if the team members, the Scrum master, and the product owner already have the right skills and abilities to create the product. Scrum is not a magical set of rules that any organization could just follow like a cookbook recipe and expect instant results. What I've given you is a basic understanding on the essentials of Scrum and how to use it to tap into the skills of the team members, Scrum master, and product owner, turning those into powerful leverages in creating innovative products on time.

Scrum is flexible in a sense that after several projects, it can morph into a completely different framework, perhaps with more effective tools, artifacts, and roles. Nevertheless, Scrum has no marked finish line. There is no end goal that means you can stop learning.

Being good in the implementation of Scrum is never the end goal of companies. In the same way that studying is not the end goal of students, rather, to learn more effectively, learning to be more proficient with Scrum means you'll be able to help your company reach its goal better.

Some methodologies actually have end states, which is why they have certain levels to reach. Scrum, however, does not make an assumption that there is a state wherein you can no longer transcend the current state. It assumes that you will always find new and better ways of achieving goals. After all, this is the real world, where the best does not stay the best for too long.

No Such Thing as a Perfect Start

I've probably mentioned this quite a few times in this book one way or another, but that's because a lot of people still can't quite get this concept right. A lot of people try to implement Scrum, only to delay the start of implementation because they can't seem to perfect the concepts of Scrum. Ironically, this is exactly what Scrum is against: waiting for the perfect moment before you begin.

We live in a non-ideal world. Ideal conditions only exist in abstract mathematical notations that only a few of us would live to see. Scrum allows changes to happen because of the fact that people who try to implement Scrum will inevitably make mistakes before, during, and after the development process. A team's concept of perfection before product development will inevitably be different from their concept of perfection during and after.

If you're worried that you don't have everything perfectly planned, you should stop worrying! Perfection means no longer being able to learn new things, and Scrum emphasizes the need to continuously learn and grow. In most cases, the first few sprints may be somewhat disappointing or even downright ugly, but that's all right. The important thing is that the succeeding sprints start to become better than the previous ones, and in most cases, they really will.

Get started! By starting as soon as you can, you give your company a lot of time to grow.

The first few sprints won't be perfect and neither would the sprints in the distant future, but no Scrum implementation is ever problem-proof. All companies have problems implementing Scrum. Remember that since Scrum helps companies discover hidden kinks and bottlenecks, the companies that find these problems may associate difficulties from the problems to the Scrum framework itself. This misconception is understandable because a lot of methodologies sometimes make work seem a lot easier than it is by hiding potential problems, only to let them pop-up somewhere near the end.

Scrum is a bit more thorough, letting the teams see potential problems ahead in the beginning, middle, and end of the production. The thing is, though, Scrum doesn't tell you how to solve those problems. It can only tell you so much; the Scrum master, product owner, and team member all have to work together to find a solution.

I've said before that one can change some aspects of Scrum should he find more effective solutions, but beware that a lot of people tend to change Scrum, thinking that it'd lead to more efficient operations only to find out that they were slowly reverting back to their old methodologies. If there are dysfunctional people in the organization, the introduction of such a powerful framework that exposes bottlenecks, kinks, and other problems may make them rebellious to the idea of its implementation.

There will be a lot of impediments especially in problematic organizations before Scrum could be implemented. It takes patience, consistency, and diligence to properly cement the foundations of Scrum into a weakly managed organization. A lot of people, even the ones with good intentions, will rebel. People naturally resist change, especially ones that force them to change their way of thinking. Help the people involved by easing them into the principles of Scrum and give them a concrete view of the goals you're trying to achieve through this change in methodology and framework. The more the people understand Scrum, the less they'll resist its implementation. The less people who resist new implementations, the better your company will be at implementing Scrum.

I don't claim that this book has all the answers you'll ever need. Far from that, I encourage you to keep learning and keep asking questions. Keep challenging existing ideologies in a healthy manner. I hope that this book has given you a lot of insights and ideas about the Scrum framework to help you in your journey in creating and delivering great and innovative software. Good luck and may your visions for your company and your teams come true!

Appendix

The following values and principles originally appeared on http://agilemanifesto.org and is included in its entirety.

Manifesto for Agile Software Development

We are uncovering better ways of developing software by doing it and helping others do it. Through this work we have come to value:

Individuals and interactions over processes and tools
Working software over comprehensive documentation
Customer collaboration over contract negotiation
Responding to change over following a plan

That is, while there is value in the items on the right, we value the items on the left more.

Kent Beck
Mike Beedle
Arie van Bennekum
Alistair Cockburn
Ward Cunningham
Martin Fowler
James Grenning
Jim Highsmith
Andrew Hunt
Ron Jeffries
Jon Kern

Brian Marick
Robert C. Martin
Steve Mellor
Ken Schwaber
Jeff Sutherland
Dave Thomas

Principles behind the Agile Manifesto

We follow these principles:

Our highest priority is to satisfy the customer
through early and continuous delivery
of valuable software.

Welcome changing requirements, even late in
development. Agile processes harness change for
the customer's competitive advantage.

Deliver working software frequently, from a
couple of weeks to a couple of months, with a
preference to the shorter timescale.

Business people and developers must work
together daily throughout the project.

Build projects around motivated individuals.
Give them the environment and support they need,
and trust them to get the job done.

The most efficient and effective method of
conveying information to and within a development
team is face-to-face conversation.

Working software is the primary measure of progress.

Agile processes promote sustainable development.
The sponsors, developers, and users should be able
to maintain a constant pace indefinitely.

Continuous attention to technical excellence
and good design enhances agility.

Simplicity--the art of maximizing the amount
of work not done--is essential.

The best architectures, requirements, and designs
emerge from self-organizing teams.

At regular intervals, the team reflects on how
to become more effective, then tunes and adjusts
its behavior accordingly.

Other Books by the Author

C# Programming for Beginners
http://www.linuxtrainingacademy.com/c-sharp

C# is a simple and general-purpose object-oriented programming language. Combine this with its versatility and huge standard library it's easy to see why it's such a popular and well-respected programming language.

When you learn how to program in C# you will be able to develop web based applications or graphical desktop applications. One of the best things about C# is that it's easy to learn... especially with this book.

Java Programming
http://www.linuxtrainingacademy.com/java-programming

Java is one of the most widely used and powerful computer programming languages in existence today. Once you learn how to program in Java you can create software applications that run on servers, desktop computers, tablets, phones, Blu-ray players, and more.

Also, if you want to ensure your software behaves the same regardless of which operation system it runs on, then Java's "write once, run anywhere" philosophy is for you. Java was design to be platform independent allowing you to create applications that run on a variety of operating systems including Windows, Mac, Solaris, and Linux.

JavaScript: A Guide to Learning the JavaScript Programming Language
http://www.linuxtrainingacademy.com/javascript

JavaScript is a dynamic computer programming language that is commonly used in web browsers to control the behavior of web pages and interact with users. It allows for asynchronous communication and can update parts of a web page or even replace the entire content of a web page. You'll see JavaScript being used to display date and time information, perform animations on a web site, validate form input, suggest results as a user types into a search box, and more.

Disclaimer and Terms of Use: Effort has been made to ensure that the information in this book is accurate and complete. However, the author and the publisher do not warrant the accuracy of the information, text and graphics contained within the book due to the rapidly changing nature of science, research, known and unknown facts. The author and the publisher do not hold any responsibility for errors, omissions, or contrary interpretation of the subject matter herein. This book is presented solely for informational purposes only.